IMPORTANT!
READ THIS!

Business books are boring. Period. BORING!

So, I have wrapped this topic in humor. This book is meant to be funny, but also meant to convey an important point... most managers are really big jerks.

If you received this book as an anonymous gift... you are a jerk! Just accept it, learn from it and read on. (Insert laugh here.)

Maybe you are a new manager and want to avoid being a jerk. This book will give you a tip each day to help you be the best manager you can be. (Insert slight smile here.)

Read one tip each day or use this book as a guide for your team.

Read on... The first step to success is to admit you just might be a jerk.

©2008 ©2009

Ryan Robert Dohrn and Brain Swell Media LLC

Published by Brain Swell Media LLC

www.BrainSwellMedia.com

All rights reserved. Printed in the United States of America.
Except as permitted under the United States copyright act of 1976,
no part of this publication may be reproduced, stored in a retrieval system,
or transmitted in any form or by any means electronic, mechanical,
photocopying, recording or otherwise without the prior
permission of the publisher.

ISBN 978-0-557-20753-4

Dedication

*To Guy, Stan, Michael, Tom and JD…
you were the managers who I admired over the years.
I learned a ton from each of you. You are not jerks.*

*To all those other managers, general managers,
sales managers, senior producers and want-to-be managers
in my career who were really big jerks
(yes, you were a jerk) . . . you helped me learn
how to be a great manager.*

*To the best manager of them all, my wife Andre' —
you can harass me any day!*

HOW TO BE A MANAGER
WITHOUT BEING A JERK

365 Tips To Being A Great Manager Every Day

by
Ryan Robert Dohrn

Table Of Contents

Tips 1-50 13

Character Test #1 23

Tips 51-100 27

Character Test #2 35

Tips 101-150 39

Character Test #3 47

Tips 151-200 51

Character Test #4 59

Tips 201-250 63

Character Test #5 71

Tips 251-300 75

Character Test #6 85

Tips 301-365 89

Final Exam 101

The Jerk Test

*Answer honestly. If you try and beat this test… you are a jerk!
To get the most out of this book, be honest with yourself
and strive to learn from your mistakes.*

QUESTION #1: Do you make most of your phone calls, in your office, on your speaker phone? If your answer is yes, give yourself 5 points. If your answer is no, give yourself 10 points.

Score: __10__

QUESTION #2: What is your preferred type of communication with your staff? If your answer is email, give yourself 5 points. If your answer is phone, give yourself 5 points. If your answer is face-to-face, give yourself 10 points.

Score: __5__

QUESTION #3: Do you know the names of the spouse of each employee you supervise? If your answer is no, give yourself 5 points. If your answer is yes, give yourself 10 points.

Score: __5__

QUESTION #4: Do you make a new pot of coffee when you either (a) drink the last cup or (b) there is not enough for another cup? If your answer is no, give yourself 5 points. If your answer is yes, give yourself 10 points.

Score: __5__

Now, add up your points….　　　　　　　　　Final Score: __25__

NOTE:
If you are using this book as a group training guide,
answer these questions on your own and
then discuss them as a group.
Be open, honest and SHARE.

First, did you try and beat the test?
If so, just skip to tip number one on page 12 and
start reading because you are a jerk.
Second, if you skipped the test, turn to tip number one
on page 12 and start reading because you are a jerk too.

Jerk Test Results

20 POINTS OR BELOW:

If you scored below 20 points, this book is for you.

20-25 POINTS:

If you scored 20-25 points you still need this book.

30 POINTS OR MORE:

If you scored 30 or above, rest assured this book will take you from being a solid manager to a great manager.

Tips 1-50

Ready, Set,

GROW!

1. Great managers have their office doors open more often than closed. A Fortune 500 CEO once removed all his senior managers' doors for one month to prove this point. Ask yourself, why am I closing my door?

2. In an effort to better understand your employees, listen to them. All too often managers have some great advice and "tune out" the employee as they wait to pounce with advice. Begin better practices of listening to employees. But, when you engage in the great practice of listening, you need to do so in an effort to better understand. Do not listen to just listen. Listening without seeking to better your understanding is like listening to a beautiful song and not hearing the melody.

3. Communicate, communicate, communicate. Rarely are managers scolded because they communicate too often to their team.

4. Reward loyalty with as much as you can give. There is nothing, NOTHING more important than being loyal to your team and teaching them to be loyal as well.

5. Take the time to say "good morning" to each person who works under you, and mean it. As you move up the "ladder" the number of people becomes larger, and this task becomes more important than ever.

6. Quarterly team meetings are an excellent way to let your team know what is going on with your company. Do this in person

with the staff. Be honest and point out great wins, but not people in particular. If you do single someone out, be prepared to continue this practice with others; be sure you are consistent or others will feel left out.

7   Be careful about brainstorming in the midst of a conversation with your team. Your brainstorming may be interpreted as orders or directives to be accomplished. In addition, be careful with words like, "we are going to" and "we will create."

8   Many managers suffer from SPIT (Smartest Person Is Talking Syndrome). More often than not, the manager does all the talking. This is seen by others in different ways. Most often, it is interpreted as the manager thinks he's the smartest person in the room. Everyone hates the smartest person in the room. Work hard to guide conversations and not do all the talking.

9   Involve your team in the hiring process. Often, the manager will be the only person involved in the hiring of a new employee. The resentment will begin from day one toward the new employee because the rest of the team feels that this new person has been forced upon them or chosen only by you. Establish a hiring system that involves the rest of the team and you'll see a dramatic change in how the new hire is accepted into the group.

10 Giving compliments that are only intended to gain favor are quickly discovered and will come back to haunt you later.

11 Gossip will kill your team. *"Who gossips to you will gossip of you"* is an appropriate Turkish proverb. First, manage gossip by not being a gossip yourself. Second, demand that gossip come to an end. Explain how gossip has a negative impact on the team. Finally, listen carefully to the subject matter surrounding the gossip. You may be able to extinguish the gossip by simply communicating better with your team.

12 Show some pride in your company and logo. Order nice shirts and hats for the team and give them away on employment anniversaries or holidays. Not t-shirts, but rather nice polo type or button-up shirts.

13 If times are rough, do not hide it from the team. Get them involved in fixing the problem. Work harder and smarter.

14 Children need to be lectured to make sure that they get your point; the same point may be stated in many repetitive ways. Adults do not learn this way. The more you lecture the less effective your point. Be firm, clear and concise. Do not lecture an adult under any circumstance.

15 One of the most common things said about managers is that they love to hear themselves talk. This is very true, and very wrong. Some of the best Fortune 500 CEOs will tell you that they ask questions and let others talk. Guide conversations, do not "be" the conversation. If you have hired the right people, reduce your stress by allowing them to solve the problem.

16 Take time each day to ask key people if they need you for anything.

17 Taking the time to "just catch up" is meaningless. Do not waste an employee's time.

18 Using wall-sized calendars is a great way to keep your staff informed about tasks and keep them on track. Use various marker colors for various departments.

19 If sales are off, stop and think about the issue. Often, you can think yourself out of a jam rather than just working harder to sell more.

20 Be mindful when you call someone to your office. It is sort of like being called to the principal's office in school. Be specific when you ask someone to come to your office. For example, "Bob, can you come to my office for a really quick chat about project X."

21 Consultants are an excellent way to have others point out the obvious. But, do not use consultants to validate your unpopular views.

22 Do not close your office door when the meeting you're having is not private. Train people when and how to interrupt you and you will not have to close your door. Remember, a great manager will have their door open more often than closed.

23   Do not conduct all your calls on your speakerphone. One significant sign of vanity or egotism is the boss who conducts every call on his speakerphone for the whole world to hear.

24   There is no such thing as a confidential conversation. Nasty divorces prove that even your spouse will not take your darkest secret to the grave. Assume that anything and everything you say will be repeated.

25   Involve your team in the budget process. Ask them for input, rather than just delivering them numbers they have to live with after the budget is approved.

26   Keep consultants at a distance. You want to pluck their ideas like apples from a tree.

27   E-mail communication lacks tone, voice, and cannot accurately communicate your emotions. Unless you are Stephen King, do not expect an e-mail to express your feelings. Chats in person are much better.

28   Read your e-mails before you hit send. Errors in grammar and spelling are common, as e-mail is supposed to be an informal communication method.

29   Hold select meetings in the break room.

30   Ask for volunteers to be on your next project rather than pick who you think is best.

31   When setting up and defining a project, ask for daily updates via e-mail to avoid micro-managing the project.

32   Potentially controversial changes in policy should be delivered in person to the team. The level of respect you receive from an employee is often based on how you handle these types of situations.

33   You do not need to know your employees' children's birthdays, but you do need to know the names of their children and spouses.

34   Create the discipline to write weekly updates to your boss and your staff. Include the good, the bad, and the ugly. Have you ever heard someone say, "Wow, the boss sure keeps us informed — what a pain"?

35   You will never hear from an employee, "I sure wish the boss would keep us in the dark." Updates about projects are critical to your success as a manager. Lack of communication is the single most quoted reason that employees are unhappy.

36   Set an agenda for every meeting and stick to it.

37   Do not eat your employees' food from the fridge.

38 Do not talk about employees with other employees no matter the circumstance.

39 Yell only once per year. It will mean more when you do.

40 Schedule employee reviews in your Outlook® calendar and do not miss the reviews. Do them yearly.

41 Meetings are a waste of time if they are not set up for success. Have a very specific reason to meet and then do so diligently.

42 Always be clear about the tasks you are giving an employee. Set a timeline and follow up often to be sure the task is on track. Ask the employee to repeat your request back to you.

43 Take each member of your team out to lunch once per year. Make it very informal. No big announcement.

44 Avoid micro-management by being very clear with each project up front and setting short deadlines. This allows you to monitor the project and not appear to be a micro-manager.

45 On Fridays, ask for a short report that tells what happened that week and what is on the agenda for next week. Monday is not the day to gather around and figure out your week. By then, you should be working. In addition, if you discuss things on Friday, employees will have time to think about the project over the weekend and come back with fresh ideas.

46 Take a break for yourself. Lead by example. Walks around the block are good for you and for your team. Get some air, let off some steam.

47 Ask for a window on your door so that people can see inside, eliminating any possibility of rumors. Sorry, your naps are up for review now.

48 You are the boss, so if you are leaving early tell the team. Do not make up an excuse. They will find out and you will look foolish.

49 Time clocks are for factories. Demand discipline, define office hours, set a good example and arrive early.

50 No chairs in a room does not a shorter meeting make. No chairs means angry employees who feel like you are playing games. Further to this point, be wary of management gimmicks you read online. Remember the age-old saying: *"If it sounds too good to be true…."* I would encourage you to set a meeting agenda, stick to the agenda, and have shorter meetings.

Character Test #1

QUESTION #1: Do you feel that your office door is a barrier of privilege? If your answer is yes, give yourself 5 points. If your answer is no, give yourself 10 points.

Score: __10__

QUESTION #2: Do you talk more than your staff in most meetings? If your answer is yes, give yourself 5 points. If your answer is no, give yourself 10 points.

Score: __5__

QUESTION #3: When times are tough, do you insulate your team? If your answer is yes, give yourself 5 points. If your answer is no, give yourself 10 points.

Score: __5__

QUESTION #4: Do you make a new pot of coffee when you either (a) drink the last cup or (b) there is not enough for another cup? If your answer is no, give yourself 5 points. If your answer is yes, or "I will start tomorrow…" give yourself 10 points.

Score: __5__

Now, add up your points…. Final Score: __25__

SCORE:

20 or less: Keep reading.

25-30: You are learning.

35-40: Keep up the good work.

NOTE:
If you are using this book as a group training guide,
answer these questions on your own and
then discuss them as a group.
Be open, honest and SHARE.

Bonus Tip

Work smarter and you will survive longer than working harder.
While hard work is a core business principle,
smart work is critical to your long-term success.
A perfect example is the homebuilder who refused
to hire a bigger crew for fear that the home's construction
would lose quality. His competitor hired a solid foreman
who trained under him for several months.
He checked on the crew and foreman religiously,
and set numerous measures in place to check for quality.
He then had more time to bid projects
and grew his business tenfold.

Tips 51–100

The secret to being

a great manager

is in the details.

51 Stop sitting at the end of the table at meetings and lunch. Try the middle of the table instead.

52 Be brief in staff meetings. Brevity is the spice of life. Masters of brevity are some of the most powerful people in the world.

53 Stock the bathroom with quality reading material. Keep it business-oriented.

54 Invest in good coffee and half-and-half. Bad coffee and powdered creamer are not a good way to pump people up for a long day's work.

55 Get your folks involved with a local charity like Habitat For Humanity. Work on-site with them. No excuses. Everyone helps.

56 Schedule off-site gatherings that are not work related. Endeavor to grow a fraternal feeling within your group.

57 Do not become guilty of paralysis by analysis. Make a decision, darn it.

58 If you have an issue with one employee, talk to him or her, and do not send out a mass e-mail to the entire team.

59 Having fewer meetings does not increase efficiency. Better meetings that are well-prepared and laid out increase efficiency.

60   Everybody hates a scrooge. Do not be pennywise and cut things that are important to your team. Switching pens from Brand A to Brand B saves ten cents per pen. But Brand B pens are messy and uncomfortable.

61   Schedule a question-and-answer session once per quarter. Take questions in advance and be to-the-point with your answers.

62   Reward great suggestions with a cash bonus. Suggestion boxes are not a thing of the past.

63   Be wary of mass e-mails about announcements. Too many questions will come up, so hold a meeting instead.

64   Do not let the same people sit to your right or to your left at every meeting.

65   Share the financials with your team. If the ship is sinking, don't you want to know?

66   When asked to keep something confidential, respect the request, even if you feel the matter does not deserve the top-secret status that was requested.

67   Create a "Great Idea Pool." Each time a member of the team brings a great idea to the table place $5 in the pool. Make the pool goal a dollar amount written on a white board or bulletin

board in a public area. Once the pool reaches that amount, buy pizza for the team or donate the money to charity. Reward great ideas.

68 Just because you think Secretary's Day is a stupid holiday does not mean that the Office Manager thinks it is stupid. Take the time to buy some flowers and say, "You are so much more than a secretary around here, so here is a small token of our thanks for all you do."

69 Do not drink the last cup of coffee without making a new pot.

70 Corporate credit cards can kill your budget and give your employees a false sense of entitlement. For as long as you can, avoid corporate cards where the company pays the bill. When employees use their own credit cards and are quickly reimbursed, they watch their expenditures much more closely. Be sure to have a fast reimbursement system as well, to ensure that a prolonged payment does not reflect poorly on your employees' credit ratings.

71 Buy enough birthday cards for your staff at one time each year and keep them hidden in your desk. Give them out on the special day and write a nice note.

72 Buy thank you cards and use them. The written word is a lost art form.

73   Democracies rarely hold relevance in the workplace. Get input, but make it clear that you make the decisions.

74   Place chairs for guests beside your desk in your office, or flip your desk around so that you are not looking over it at others when having a conversation.

75   Do not be afraid to make a wrong decision. If you end up being wrong, admit it.

76   Be interruptible. Always be prepared to answer a question or give advice. When you are gruff about being interrupted then your people will fear asking for help.

77   Ruling by fear went out with the Knights of the Round Table. Fear will get you nowhere in managing others.

78   Turn meetings into briefings. Briefings imply what length of time the meeting should be… brief.

79   Respect will always glean better returns on your investment in your team.

80   Get to know your employees personally, but do not get personal with your employees.

81   Train your employees to train others. Teach your methods once, so that others can teach your methods many times over.

82 Saving money is one thing, but sharing a hotel room with someone under you, especially someone of the opposite sex, is another. This seems obvious, but it comes up often, especially with younger and newer employees who think they are just following orders. Even if "nothing happens," this is the worst of the worst.

83 Become aware of how thin the walls of your office truly are. Do a small test with a fellow employee who you trust. Some managers run a small radio or TV in the background to cover up the noise of a conversation. Remember, every member of your team has a right to privacy when speaking with you.

84 We all screw up. Sometimes we repeat something that we were asked to keep confidential because we feel that it is "not a biggie." Admit this error to the person who asked you to keep the secret. Explain that you screwed up and tell them that you fully understand that they most likely will never tell you anything confidential again. If it was a "slip of the tongue," then admit it, and if you just flat out blew it, admit that too.

85 Organizational charts create problems, so keep them hidden. Having an organizational chart is great for budgeting, planning and overall strategy, but posting it in the break room is one of the worst things I have ever observed.

86 Do not hire your friends. Nothing you can do will ever make your friend a "normal" employee with the rest of your team. Nothing.

87 Stop blaming your boss because you are afraid to make a hard decision.

88 Do not answer your phone during a meeting. You have set time aside for the meeting, so observe the time and honor the person in your office with your attention.

89 Do not answer your phone during an employee evaluation.

90 Always, always be kind to the mailman, UPS lady or the FedEx guy. Always!

91 Teach your employees when to ask you hard questions. Train them to your clock for best results.

92 E-mails longer than three paragraphs are a waste of your time. E-mail is supposed to be used as an informal communication tool. Write a letter in Word and attach it to an e-mail. Use proper form in writing your letter, as if you were sending it in the mail.

93 Set up weekly briefings with key people and make them and yourself stick to the day and time. Do not allow the time to float. Create discipline.

94 Ask about pet peeves when you interview a new hire. Make a note of these on their resume for future reference.

95 Share your pet peeves with new employees. Train them from day one how to manage you.

96 "Secretary" is old school and sounds old school, try "personal assistant" for an ego boost to your right-hand employee.

97 Place the copier in a convenient, yet concealed, location. A noisy copier running all day is very annoying. Also, constant traffic to the copier is a major distraction to those near the copier. Take some time to consider these things when locating this important piece of equipment.

98 Offer table lamps to your team. Overhead fluorescent lights give off a sterile, hospital-like hue to an office.

99 Install full-length mirrors in sales peoples' offices. Sales people sell better when they can see themselves.

100 Never deliver bad news on Friday. Ask yourself, is there a reason to ruin this person's weekend?

Character Test #2

QUESTION #1: Do you meet with your team weekly? If your answer is yes, give yourself 10 points. If your answer is no, give yourself 5 points.

Score: _____

QUESTION #2: Have you hired a personal friend to work under you? If your answer is yes, give yourself 5 points. If your answer is no, give yourself 10 points.

Score: _____

QUESTION #3: When having a drink with the team after work, are you the first one to leave? If your answer is yes, give yourself 10 points. If your answer is no, give yourself 5 points.

Score: _____

QUESTION #4: Do you have your office door open more than it is closed? If your answer is no, give yourself 5 points. If your answer is yes, or "I will start tomorrow…" give yourself 10 points.

Score: _____

Now, add up your points…. Final Score: _____

SCORE:

20 or less: Keep reading.

25-30: You are learning.

35-40: Keep up the good work

NOTE:
If you are using this book as a group training guide,
answer these questions on your own and
then discuss them as a group.
Be open, honest and SHARE.

Bonus Tip

If you set a time to chat with an employee,
be on time for the meeting.
The employee will be upset for 24 hours before this meeting
and every minute you are late makes the situation worse.
If you forget the meeting they will be upset until you remember.
Value an employee's time as much as you
value your own time.
Be punctual or send communication
that you will be delayed.

Tips 101 – 150

After falling off...

finding the nerve

to get back on the horse

is where the true lesson begins.

101 Break the habit of calling people on your drive home. Being the last call of the day is not fun and makes your team feel like you forgot them. Use that time to relax or call your mom.

102 No one likes being called to the boss's office. Go to their office, desk or cubicle to chat.

103 Insist that your team takes breaks.

104 Insist that your employees take their vacation days.

105 Get your team involved from day one. People are more passionate when they are involved from the beginning of a project.

106 Make your expectations clear and do not change them mid-course. Keep your expectations simple and do not expand your list without reason. Clear communication is very important to the growth of your team.

107 E-mail is no way to hand down a punishment. Have a personal conversation and then document the conversation.

108 Make sure employees sign all written notices of their discipline.

109 Develop an MVP awards program. Stick to it. Ask for nominations from your team each month. Reward with a plaque and lunch with the boss.

110 After-work drinks are fine; just be sure you are one of the first to depart. Always leave more money than the amount you owe for food and drink.

111 Pick up the bill for lunch and do not make it a big deal. A gentle, "I got this one... keep up the good work" goes a long way. Do not flaunt expense accounts.

112 Take a walk around the block and invite an employee along for the stroll. Ask about their hobbies.

113 Long meetings are often poorly planned meetings. Set clear goals and objectives before the meeting begins.

114 Never scold an employee in front of others. Very rarely will belittling anyone help to make your point.

115 Be fair yet firm. Five minutes late is not the end of the world.

116 Make sure your expectations match the pay scale. Why does everyone expect good service at a fast food restaurant being run by a minimum wage crew?

117 Take your team to the movies. A break from the norm is good for the brain. Do not expect all employees to say thank you. Remember the ones who do and privately tell them how much you appreciated that.

118 Buy great office chairs and do not skimp. Remember, often the best chairs are not the most expensive.

119 Hold a monthly drawing for the best parking spot in the lot. Employees can only win once per year or however many months to make sure that everyone has a chance to win.

120 Have pizza brought in for lunch one day. No glory, just pizza. Don't forget cheese-only or veggie pizza too.

121 Ask for feedback and be prepared to get it. It's often hard to just sit and listen. Take notes. Let them know that you're paying attention. Do not defend yourself. Just listen. It may be the hardest thing you do today.

122 Create a suggestion box and be prepared to take the good with the bad. The bigger step forward is to then act on the suggestions.

123 Be predictable with your office hours.

124 Heed the old saying, *"Slow and easy wins the race."* Why do so few managers apply this principle?

125 Tell others when you are leaving the office, when you will return, and how they can get a hold of you while you are out.

126 Change your voicemail when you are out of town and change it back when you return.

127 Cute voicemail messages are for children. Be straightforward and honest. Are you in or out? When will you return your calls?

128 Return all calls to salespeople in 48 hours or less. Be blunt and tell them you are not interested, but call them back.

129 If you know it is right, do it. If you know it is wrong, do not do it. If you do not know, ask. Teach this system daily to your team.

130 Do not keep a bad employee out of fear that you cannot replace them.

131 Never let your employees see you sweat in a crisis. Just imagine if the Captain of a sinking ship said, "Ah crap y'all, we better jump off this booger or we'll all die."

132 Never be afraid to fire the wrong person.

133 Never consume more than two drinks of alcohol at a company function. Never allow the company to buy alcohol. Never have your picture taken with a drink in your hand. Be wary of photographers at functions where alcohol is being consumed. Never be afraid to pay for a cab for a fellow employee who cannot drive home after consuming too much alcohol.

134 Always have tissues ready if you are going to deliver bad news to an employee.

135 It is the "little people" in life who will come to the rescue when you are in a pinch. What do you do each day to make them feel important or special?

136 Always set goals that are realistic. All too often managers set the goal of reaching the moon knowing full well that the top of the trees is perfectly fine. Why not help your people reach reasonable goals and then celebrate?

137 Always send flowers when an employee loses a close relative.

138 When planning staff outings, give choices for activities. Not everyone likes softball or volleyball.

139 Never have an employee of the opposite sex in your office with the door closed for more than thirty minutes.

140 Ask key people for a weekly update. Do not do week-in-review reports on Friday. Things that have already happened are too late to manage. Ask for a "what's up this week" update by 10am Monday morning.

141 If an employee of the opposite sex is dressed inappropriately at work, speak to him or her in private while another employee of the same sex is within view.

142 When delivering bad news, have a witness in the room of the same sex as the person receiving the bad news. Make it a person they like if you can.

143 Have a different dress policy for each season. Allow employees to participate in the planning of this program. Encourage employees to be professional yet comfortable.

144 Hold all your key meetings on one day. Mondays work very well as this gives you a full week to complete tasks. Plan these meetings in advance and schedule them weekly. Create discipline.

145 Low employee turnover rates are not necessarily a good thing. Too much of a bad thing can often be hidden under an HR statistic.

146 Install a whiteboard in your break room for a joke of the day. Make sure that "G-rated only" is clearly posted. For example: "Why can't you play poker in the jungle? Because there are too many cheetahs."

147 Make a big deal about victories, no matter how small.

148 Place a bell in the center of the office for the sales people to ring when a sale is completed.

149 Play Pictionary® once per year with your team. This encourages team work and is fun too.

150 Pass on what you learn. Training the people around you makes your job easier and helps them advance in their careers. Rarely do people become millionaires by doing everything themselves. Get help, rely on help, but in the end, own it.

Character Test #3

QUESTION #1: Do you celebrate each sale as a win for the whole team? If your answer is yes, give yourself 10 points. If your answer is no, give yourself 5 points.

Score: _____

QUESTION #2: Do you ask for weekly reports or "what's up next week" reports? If your answer is "weekly" give yourself 5 points. If your answer is "next week" give yourself 10 points.

Score: _____

QUESTION #3: Do you deliver bad news on Fridays? If your answer is yes, give yourself 5 points. If your answer is no, give yourself 10 points.

Score: _____

QUESTION #4: Do you know the mail carrier's name? If your answer is no, give yourself 5 points. If your answer is yes, or "I will ask tomorrow…" give yourself 10 points.

Score: _____

Now, add up your points….   Final Score: _____

SCORE:

20 or less: Keep reading.

25-30: You are learning.

35-40: Keep up the good work.

NOTE:
If you are using this book as a group training guide, answer these questions on your own and then discuss them as a group.
Be open, honest and SHARE.

Bonus Tip

Set yourself up for success.
Create a litmus test to gauge employee ideas.
Employees can then run their ideas through this test
before bringing them to you.

1. Does the idea match our customer?
2. Does the idea grow revenue?
3. Does the idea help us grow our mission statement?
4. Does the idea support our core objectives?
5. Does the cost of the idea balance with revenue potential?

To make these gauges work you will need to know
your core demographic, have a mission statement
and have core business objectives.
Missing these things? Get going!

Tips 151–200

Once you start, finish.

If you fail, don't just try again.

First, figure out why you failed

the first time.

Then, try again.

151   At company functions, never pit managers against employees in games.

152   Office politics are tough. Do not play games with others. Be straight-forward and honest. Mind games rarely yield positive results.

153   Create a handwritten thank you note for an employee who has done something extra special. Keep it simple and direct. Show you noticed and you care.

154   Play fun, up-tempo music from 4pm until close on Friday. End the week on a positive note.

155   Set a realistic budget so that you can celebrate wins rather than trying to reach numbers that require whipping your team all year long.

156   Set a good example and keep your out-of-office lunches short. When lunching with an employee make it a point to get back to work in under an hour.

157   Offer bottled water or a water filter on the tap in the break room. Encourage employees to drink plenty of water.

158   Be a family friendly work zone. Be flexible and let your team know that it is ok to take care of family business. But also be

firm about the employee making up the missed work. Avoid issues by setting your policies in advance. Coming in early to make the time up is better than staying late. After-hours work is often wasted time.

159 Allowing employees to work after hours is not very smart. Ask them to come in early if they want to leave early the next day.

160 Encourage flu shots and healthy living.

161 It is not better to ask forgiveness later than for permission first. This is by far one of the dumbest things ever said by a manager. It's even worse to hear one of your team say this to a fellow employee about you.

162 Healthy employees are happy employees. Do all you can to keep your people healthy. Form a healthy workforce committee to provide ideas about what you can do to keep the workplace healthy and happy.

163 Blood drives are an excellent way to encourage charity within your team. Ask for a volunteer to help you get the drive set up.

164 Do not get a nicer hotel room than your employees when you travel, no matter your rank within the company.

165 Always ask to assist fellow employees with their bags when traveling. Never allow your employees to carry your bags. Even if they ask to help, the end result is that they carried the boss's bags.

166 Be very clear with your travel policies. Every detail is important, even how many alcoholic drinks, if any, may be purchased on the company credit card.

167 Company issued credit cards, while a bit easier to manage, will always result in increased expenses. Employees who use their own credit cards for travel are much more likely to treat expenses like their own.

168 Never deliver bad news via voicemail.

169 Form a book club in your office. Stock the club with books about various aspects of your business.

170 Allowing employees to work from home is an excellent perk, but there are some jobs that just cannot be done from home. Thus, you need to be fair to everyone and not allow working from home at all. Or, allow it on a very limited basis.

171 Read, read, read. Keep up-to-date on current trends in all aspects of your business. Subscribe to industry newsletters online and set aside time each week for research.

172 Position your desk in such a way that your back is not to the door.

173 Set up an internal arbitration committee for resolving internal employee conflicts. Make it very clear that conflicts should try to be worked out between those involved first. If no resolution is reached, then the arbitration committee will get involved.

174 Bringing interpersonal employee issues to a quick resolution is very important.

175 Use mood lighting to make your office comfortable and inviting to your team. You want your team to feel comfortable in your office.

176 Choose a chair that is at the same level as the other chairs in your office. It is an old-school idea that the boss should sit in a chair that is higher than the employees as a way to show that the boss is in a position of power.

177 Do not confide in employees about your personal information, issues, or family business.

178 Stories, anecdotes, or analogies are a great way to explain your point. But, be sure your team will understand the analogy. Relating your team's failures to your local sports team's failures only works if your employees know what the heck you are talking about. Be careful that your analogies do not make your point even harder to grasp.

179 Do not give alcohol as a gift to employees.

180 No matter your religious beliefs, encourage an Angel tree project near the holiday season. This is where an employee or group of employees buys Christmas gifts for low-income children.

181 Every idea is valid. Do not extinguish any idea. It is better to bank an idea and say, "Not a bad idea, let me make note of that…" than to say, "Huh, bad idea, no way. Where did that come from?" Just because an employee had a bad idea today does not mean that tomorrow their next idea might not make you millions. But, if you kill all ideas, then ideas will stop being offered.

182 Create a rewards program for those employees who help you find and hire great employees.

183 Buy germicide hand pump dispensers for your office. Place them in high traffic areas. Encourage employees to be germ free.

184 Do not quote company policy that is not written and has not been provided to the employee in advance.

185 Do not talk in circles. Start a thought and finish a thought. The shortest path is indeed the one that is most direct. If you have a point, make it already.

186 A nice Christmas lunch for employees only is a great alternative to a full-blown holiday party that can cost a fortune.

187 Encourage employees who travel for the company to travel on work days and not on the weekends.

188 Be a family first workplace. Make great strides to accommodate the family needs of your employees.

189 Be on the lookout for employees who tell tasteless jokes, use bad language or make inappropriate comments. Be quick to write up employees who fall into this area of concern.

190 Place a small whiteboard near your door. Make notes on that board about meetings and when you are on a conference call.

191 Get up out of your chair and go to an employee to ask even the smallest question. It is good for you and good for them. Get up and go.

192 Make your schedule available to your team. Outlook® has a great tool for this. Or, send out your schedule weekly.

193 Allow parents to bring their kids' fundraisers into work to sell. Make a policy that they can leave it on the table in the break room, but they may not sell directly to other employees.

194 Do some work yourself. Delegating is easy. Pick up a few boxes too.

195 Encourage healthy eating habits by providing utensils needed when employees bring their own lunch.

196 Knowledge is only powerful when you know how to use it. Teach them to fish and reap the rewards.

197 People love their pets, and vet appointments are often hard to schedule. Work with folks when they have a vet appointment and encourage infrequent pet visits to your office to put a smile on everyone's face.

198 Don't get lost in the process. Many managers focus so hard on the process that they forget what the end result was supposed to be. Be careful that you always are looking a long way down the road. If you focus on the dash of the car, you will not have time to watch the road and a crash will soon come.

199 Giving a compliment followed very closely by a request is very often seen as a false positive, and even more importantly, a real negative.

200 Provide small heaters or small fans to those who are climate-challenged.

Character Test #4

QUESTION #1: Do you delegate everything? If your answer is yes, give yourself 5 points. If your answer is no, give yourself 10 points.

Score: _____

QUESTION #2: Do you work on a charity project each year with your team? If your answer is yes, give yourself 10 points. If your answer is no, give yourself 5 points.

Score: _____

QUESTION #3: Do you send sick employees home without fear? If your answer is yes, give yourself 10 points. If your answer is no, give yourself 5 points.

Score: _____

QUESTION #4: Do you ever ask for volunteers rather than just assign tasks? If your answer is no, give yourself 5 points. If your answer is yes, or "I will start soon…" give yourself 10 points.

Score: _____

Now, add up your points…. Final Score: _____

SCORE:

20 or less: Keep reading.

25-30: You are learning.

35-40: Keep up the good work.

NOTE:
*If you are using this book as a group training guide,
answer these questions on your own and
then discuss them as a group.
Be open, honest and SHARE.*

Bonus Tip

When the going gets tough, the tough start asking for help.
The sign of a great leader is a person who is willing
to ask for help in a time of crisis.

True, never let them see you sweat, but don't be stupid either.
Asking for help is not admitting that you were wrong
or that you cannot handle the situation.
It is important to note that being a great manager
before the hard times, helps you get through
the tough times because any team
will help a great leader through the storm.

Tips 201-250

Learning how to be better requires that you first recognize that improvement is a good thing and not an admission of failure.

201 You never get the best from people at the end of the day. Hold tough meetings at 10am.

202 Allow your team to participate in strategic planning for the next year.

203 Never assume that you alone hold all the keys to the success of the company.

204 No one likes to be the "whipping boy." Managers often ask the person who is least resistant to do more heavy lifting. Spread out the work to everyone.

205 Get rid of the bad apples. You know the old saying. Create a path to success with the bad employee. Write it down. Have them sign it. Give them a deadline to fix their issues. If there is no progress, move them off the team.

206 Do not assume that former athletes will be great managers. For many people ego is what drove them on the field, not team work. A 90-minute game filled with raw emotion is nothing like an 8-hour day at a desk. Ask questions to determine why they loved team sports. Also, leave your sports analogies in the locker room.

207 Employee reviews are important. Do not hold a bad review on a Monday morning. Never ruin a person's weekend by presenting a bad review on a Friday. Late Monday is good. Encourage employees to ask questions the next day. Also, tell them you expect change right away.

208 Schedule a DVD break. Rent a PG-13 or G-rated movie and show it over lunch. Take a team break and you will get that time back tenfold.

209 Getting your team to agree with a decision before you make it is futile and you will be found out. Make a decision and live with the consequences. If you expect your entire team to agree with your decision, then your expectations are way off mark.

210 Give more, get more. Teach a man to fish and you will feed him for a lifetime.

211 If you ask for more from employees and they cannot do it, be sure to tell them that it is ok and that you are not disappointed. Now, if they are just being lazy, call a spade a spade.

212 Do not take excuses from anyone more than three times in a row. Set ground rules early, make them very clear and stick to them.

213 Do not encourage yelling across the office. Ask people to get up and walk over to ask a question. Do not yell from your perch either.

214 You do not always have to give advice. Sometimes people just want to talk.

215 Hold blood drives and give people a nice incentive to give blood.

216 Find a counselor you trust so you can refer your team in times of need. You might even see if the company will split the bill. Happy employees are good employees.

217 Encourage sick employees to stay home.

218 An attractive 401k plan can make up for a smaller salary.

219 Let your team go home at 3pm on days before a holiday.

220 Create "In the zone" signs for each member of your team. Have them hang this on their cubicle, back of chair, office door, etc… when they don't want to be disturbed. Tell them that they cannot leave the sign up permanently.

221 Have candy on your desk. Encourage people to take a piece. Avoid chocolate. Sugar-free? Perhaps.

222 Popcorn parties are fun. Party you say? Hand out microwave popcorn to your team. Tell them to pop it whenever they want to.

223 Never have your picture taken with an alcoholic beverage in your hand.

224 Make sure that you clearly point out who is in charge while you are on vacation. Be sure that these people know you will ask others their opinion of the job they did when you return. Loan them this book while you are away.

225 Always send flowers when employees are in the hospital, and if you can, go visit them.

226 Do not promote employees to "see" if they can handle the job. Promote an employee based on your experience that they "can" handle the job. You will kill great people by giving them a bucket of responsibility and then pulling them back when they fail.

227 Office etiquette regarding attire is a tough issue. I like to be clear from day one. This is what we wear and do not wear. If you have a question, ask me. Do not change the rules per employee or on the fly.

228 Just stop talking already! You might be the smartest guy in the room. Ok, we all get it. Stop talking. Don't be the meeting, be a part of the meeting.

229 The climb up the corporate ladder can be rough. Be careful who you step on as you climb the ladder. The "little people" will always be the ones who will bail you out in a pinch. The business world is a very small place. Create relationships and nurture those relationships for the years ahead.

230 Never mess with salespeople's commissions midstream. Give them time to re-shuffle the deck if a compensation change is coming from the top down.

231 Hire multi-talented people. Look for people with diverse backgrounds and diverse skill sets. Hiring a great writer who can also shoot pictures is a bonus. Hiring a great writer with great photography skills who can also write the code for web pages and is bi-lingual is a killer hire.

232 Update your resume on New Year's Day each year.

233 Allow your team to have music on their computers and encourage them to listen with earphones on while working. Music is a great motivator.

234 Offer cable TV in your break room. TV encourages people to take a break for lunch. You will get more work out of a well-rested person in the long haul than someone who works through lunch. Plus, there are laws about this type of issue.

235 Perhaps you are a jerk. You might want to ask a team member if the rest of the team feels this way. Take your licks and ask how you can improve.

236 Leave Post-It® thank you notes for people. A small note of thanks goes a long ways toward developing loyalty and appreciation.

237 Dress for success. Wearing a tie everyday is not needed. However, the team will follow the coach, so set a good example.

238 When writing your weekly staff update give out "kudos" to those employees who have excelled. Be sure to rotate the praise so people do not feel left out.

239 Make internal surveys a part of your bonus program. Setting up a bonus for salespeople driven by an internal survey will let the salespeople know that they better treat the internal production folks nicely or they will score them badly on the internal survey. Make the surveys anonymous and confidential. For example, a salesperson needs to score 85% or better on the internal survey to get a full bonus. Be sure to let the other employees know that this is the purpose of the survey.

240 Back up your e-mail files and big files when the seasons change. Tell your employees to do the same.

241 Plan your questions in advance when interviewing a new candidate.

242 Telling others that you have a secret you cannot share is an ego-driven way to say that the employee is not worthy of the information.

243 There is an old saying, *"You have to give respect to get respect."* Why do so few managers apply this rule?

244 Practice the 10-minute rule. Wait 10 minutes before a confrontation about any subject with an employee. Ask yourself, "Am I over reacting to this situation?" and "Does it really matter?".

245 Position your office where you can see who comes and goes. This is a subtle way to say that you are aware without being a jerk. Say "good morning" when people arrive and say "good night" and "thank you" when people leave.

246 Going to dinner with an employee and their spouse is sure to create an environment of favoritism. Avoid becoming personal friends with your employees outside of work. This will cloud your judgment.

247 Hey Mr. Grumpy, get plenty of sleep and exercise. Improved focus and concentration will help improve your efficiency so that you can complete your work in less time. Do you exercise weekly? If not... why not?

248 Encourage your team to participate in 401k plans. Show concern for this component of your employees' lives. Let them know that their future is important to you.

249 Never make a decision when you are mad. Take 24 hours to consider tough questions.

250 Create discipline with your group. Hold weekly meetings at the same time each week and ask that people be on time, every time. You need to be on time too!

Character Test #5

QUESTION #1: Do you avoid having personal friendships with those you supervise? If your answer is yes, give yourself 10 points. If your answer is no, give yourself 5 points.

Score: _____

QUESTION #2: Do you involve other members of your team in the hiring process? If your answer is no, give yourself 5 points. If your answer is yes, give yourself 10 points.

Score: _____

QUESTION #3: Do you change sales staff commissions when they start making more money than you? If your answer is yes, give yourself 5 points. If your answer is no, give yourself 10 points.

Score: _____

QUESTION #4: Do you leave thank you notes for your team on their desks? If your answer is no, give yourself 5 points. If your answer is yes, or "I will start tomorrow…" give yourself 10 points.

Score: _____

Now, add up your points….   Final Score: _____

SCORE:

20 or less: **Keep reading.**

25-30: **You are learning.**

35-40: Keep up the good work.

NOTE:
If you are using this book as a group training guide, answer these questions on your own and then discuss them as a group.
Be open, honest and SHARE.

Bonus Tip

Using wall-sized calendars is a great way
to keep your staff informed about tasks
and to keep them on track.
Place the calendar in a high traffic place,
and hold meetings near and around the calendar
for maximum performance.

Tips 251-300

Seek the counsel of the

wise people around you.

Those who history remembers

for being wise

were most often surrounded

by those wiser than themselves.

251 Be extra nice to the building security guard and the parking lot attendant. These are the people who will bail you out of a pinch one day.

252 Be on time for your appointments. Just because you are the boss does not mean that you can be late to your own meeting, or any meeting for that matter. If you are looking for a way to really crank off your staff, call a meeting and then be late. Want to really crank them off? Call a meeting and then be late because you had to make a trip to the little boys room or little girls room. Be on time. Lead by example. Demand punctuality, and demand it from yourself too.

253 Return business calls within 24 hours, or have someone else call the person back and explain your delay.

254 You should recognize employees' yearly anniversaries with your company. A card or small token of appreciation goes a long way. Plus, do not forget the employees' yearly reviews. Make it a priority. Budget for the minimum 3% raise that they all deserve.

255 Return a phone call with a phone call. Do not return a phone call with an e-mail.

256 Former jocks do not necessarily make great employees. Sure, being a team player is great. But, former sports stars are also some of the worst ego-driven maniacs in the existence of the human work force. If you are a sports nut, try not to hire more nuts. Too many nuts make a strong tree's limbs weak.

257 Good coffee is worth every penny. Do not be cheap with coffee to make your revenue/expense budget. Offer liquid creamer and sugar and make it nice. If you cannot make budget because of your expenses on coffee, you need to resign. Powdered creamer is yucky!

258 Being respectful of people's time is critical. If you say you are going to call at 2:30pm, make the call. If you are going to be late, send an e-mail. Never forget, when you as the boss set a time to meet, employees wait for the call, often not doing anything else in anxious anticipation of your call.

259 Keep your cell phone number private. That way, you are never afraid to answer it. Let employees know to only call when they need you, not just to say hello. That way, you will pick up no matter what.

260 When you cc: people on e-mail, do not expect them to reply. If you want a reply, ask for it, and put the person's name in the To: box.

261 Keep very accurate records on employee reviews, behavior, and issues. However, do not use the fact that you are keeping this file as a way to threaten the employee.

262 Giving employees a huge plate of responsibility to see what they can handle and then backing off the responsibility when they fail is very poor leadership. Give people what they can handle and then assign more as they succeed. Real jerks assign more than a person can handle to see if the person will grow to achieve the task.

263 Tell people what you want, give direction, then back off. If you have the right people on your team, they should be able to solve problems for you. Being a manager does not have to be stressful. If your people cannot solve problems, your issue may be the employees at the table.

264 Consult with your HR department often. Build a great relationship with your HR team. Learn as much as you can, and keep your employees informed.

265 Bring someone in who can explain in detail the benefits of a 401k program.

266 Buying several copies of an excellent business book for certain staff groups is a great idea. Encouraging them to read a chapter a week with you is even better. Do not expect them to read this in their off hours. If you want them to participate in your book club, give them time to read.

267 DVD training days are an excellent break from day-to-day operations. There are training DVD's for every walk of the business life. Find some online, buy them and set aside time to watch them with your team.

268 The holidays around December are a special time of year. Buying gifts can be an impossible mission. Instead, hold a Chinese gift exchange. (Google® it.) It is fun and leads more toward team building. I like to buy personal small gifts for my senior staff members. I always present the gifts to them in private. It is important to recognize your leaders, but not to make a ceremony of the process.

269 Do not have a business conversation on your cell phone within earshot of others. Excuse yourself and go someplace quiet, or tell the person you'll call them back.

270 Changing your voicemail everyday is unrealistic and not required unless you need to communicate to those calling of changes, vacation, etc.

271 Communicating important news like employee resignations is important. Even if you have nothing to share, tell the team you are working on it. Leaving people in limbo means that they are running scenarios in their own minds. Trust me, they run the wrong scenarios. Communicate even when you have nothing to communicate. Let them know you are aware that they are seeking answers.

272 Set clear goals during an employee review. Type the goals up and sign them along with your employees. Review every 60 days. What will you do to help them achieve their goals? Add their goals to your goals.

273 Set a dress code policy and stick to it. Overkill will kill your team. A mail clerk who wears a tie everyday will not be happy. Allow employees to dress appropriately for their job, but set a dress code. Do not leave interpretation up to the employee. With that said, everyone hates the "dress code police."

274 Do not expect more from your staff than others expect from you.

275 Place the fax machine near those who actually use it. Reduce traffic and noise to others. Consider eFax®.

276 Most employees will respect you for the hard decisions you make more than the small ones.

277 Ongoing training is critical to the success of your team. Budget for ongoing training and encourage your team to seek it. It is not your job to find classes for them. You cannot force an employee to learn.

278 People hate change by nature. However, do not fear change. If you present plans for change in advance and listen to the thoughts of your team, there is rarely a time that you cannot make change happen in a comfortable and positive way.

279 When making significant changes to the structure of your organization, give yourself double the transition time you think the change may take to work.

280 Same song, different verse.... Budget for coffee and bottled or filtered water. Providing both is very important to morale. This should be one of the very last things that you cut due to budget reasons. Good coffee and good water are important. Don't be cheap with these employee benefits. Good coffee equals happy employees.

281 Do not encourage donuts in the workplace. There is no greater source of sugar that you can force down your throat, besides a spoonful of sugar itself. Encouraging a healthy lifestyle is important to the success of your team.

282 Find and offer a health club benefits program. Make this plan very attractive. You will get back tenfold what you invest in a healthy employee.

283 Do not punish people who are not sick. Let employees use their sick days for healthy reasons too.

284 Dating your staff is forbidden. The dating of others within the same company can be dangerous as well. Get a gym membership and meet your next spouse at the gym or at church.

285 Never make fun of your employees. There is no such thing as poking fun just to poke fun. Practical jokes will get you fired and must be discouraged. There are hundreds of ways to show you are fun and you care, so do not make jokes about others, or you will soon find them making jokes about you. Break this habit today.

286 You cannot listen with your mouth open. Managers are very guilty of always talking and not listening. Stop talking and listen — today. Ask questions and do not be so fast to provide the solution. As with a child, if you always do all the thinking, when they leave your home, they are helpless.

287 When traveling, be wary of going out after a long day with your employees. Often you will show a side that they do not need to see. After hours is your time to rewind and unplug. Lead by example and get some rest.

288 Look at every detail of a person's appearance in an interview. The smallest details, like work shoes that are in desperate need of a polish, can give signals about future behavior.

289 Managers often feel it is easier to control employees who perceive them as friends. After all, you know them inside and out.

Not true. Personal friendships will come back to haunt you. Know your employees personally, but do not get personal.

290 Working from home is a privilege. What is fair for one is fair for all. Many jobs cannot be done at home, so be careful about this issue. There also may be HR issues.

291 Never let employees win just to make them feel better. Tiger Woods' father played to win every round of golf. Tiger beat him one day and the victory was very sweet. Argue with respect. Concede when deserved.

292 Reverse psychology is for the birds. It is easy to spot a mile away. Stop playing games and lying to your staff. Play it straight and you will get better results.

293 Call out people who roll their eyes or make funny faces in meetings. This habit is very bad in business. Be very specific and point it out. "Mary, you just rolled your eyes — did I say something that you disagree with?" Be polite. Actually, be very warm. Do this once and then make it a private conversation if it continues.

294 Decorate for the seasons and holidays. From Spring to Christmas, make the holidays or seasons special. Start a committee to decorate your office appropriately.

295 Hiring a business coach is a great way to grow your personal strength. People who use a personal trainer find themselves achieving their goals 67% more quickly.

296 The telephone is not an age-old appliance. Use it. If an e-mail takes more than 3 minutes to write, you'd be better off to just pick up the phone.

297 Call or instant message an employee; do not yell from your desk. Do not allow others to yell for people. It often is the simple things that we overlook... lead by example. Seems so simple doesn't it? Do it.

298 Even though you are the boss, always ask permission to enter an employee's office and ask if this is a good time to interrupt.

299 Be respectful of your employees' time. Ask them if they have plans before you just drop a three-hour, last-minute, needs-to-be-done-by-9am-tomorrow project on them at 4:30pm. Then, if you ask for it, do something with it. Employees hate to see the hard work they have completed go unused. If you ever catch yourself saying, "Hey, they are getting paid... they will get over it" — STOP! Rewind your internal systems. STOP! You are being a jerk! Do you value your time? Trust me, they value their time too.

300 Give the tools needed to get the job done. You are the boss, and your job is to think ahead. If you want a ten-foot hole dug in the ground in 3 days do not give your employee a spoon. Budget in advance, or do not take on the job.

Character Test #6

QUESTION #1: Do you allow "certain" employees to work from home? If your answer is no, give yourself 10 points. If your answer is yes, give yourself 5 points.

Score: _____

QUESTION #2: Do you yell from your desk to employees rather than get up? If your answer is no, give yourself 10 points. If your answer is yes, give yourself 5 points.

Score: _____

QUESTION #3: On the day before a holiday off do you TELL your employees to leave early? If your answer is yes, give yourself 10 points. If your answer is no, give yourself 5 points.

Score: _____

QUESTION #4: Do you truly listen when an employee is talking in a meeting? If your answer is no, give yourself 5 points. If your answer is yes, or "I will start tomorrow…" give yourself 10 points.

Score: _____

Now, add up your points….   Final Score: _____

SCORE:

20 or less: **Keep reading.**

25-30: **You are learning.**

35-40: **Keep up the good work.**

NOTE:
If you are using this book as a group training guide, answer these questions on your own and then discuss them as a group.
Be open, honest and SHARE.

Bonus Tip

Being indecisive is the making of a leadership disaster.
It has been said many times that any decision
is better than no decision.
If you promise a decision by a certain time,
make that time and decision a priority.

Remember, most people want a leader
and they value leadership.
If you are afraid of making the wrong decision,
then seek counsel from others.
An educated decision is often much easier to make.

Tips 301–365

If you know it is right, do it.

If you know it is wrong,

don't do it.

If you do not know if it is

right or wrong…

don't do it.

301 Check in with your office often when you travel. Ask if anyone needs to speak with you. Do not just check in when you need something.

302 While on the road, be sure your team clearly knows that they can call you on your cell phone if needed.

303 Making friends with your employees will happen no matter how hard you work against it. Be careful how you openly show your friendship in meetings and other functions. Never do weekend activities together. Never let your friendship influence your decisions. Be very clear, "At work I have to be the boss, if this does not work for you we need to not be friends."

304 Encourage your employees to get a yearly physical. Mandate that your top tier staff get quarterly physicals. Health issues are the single greatest cost of efficiency in the work place.

305 Ask for employees to share with you letters or e-mails from happy customers. Ask for their permission to circulate them around the office.

306 When asked by an employee to attend a party or gathering, do not say you will be there if you will not. DO NOT say you will try if you are not going to try. Employees pull out all the stops if they think the boss is coming to the party. When you don't show, they will remember it forever.

307 Ask your people if they want overtime. Often, people do not want or need overtime. Before you take on a new revenue-producing project that requires overtime, ask if your people are willing to do it. In some cases you will have no choice and will be forced to require overtime. But, getting buy-in from the team in advance makes them feel like part of the process.

308 People are passionate about projects that they are asked to participate in from day one. Do not drop the project bomb on someone with no clue. If you had involved them from day one, they may have been better able to handle the job and/or helped you get it done more quickly.

309 Remember the Golden Rule; it's a no brainer. It is so simple, yet very rarely applied by managers.

310 Never, ever call an employee when you are angry. Give yourself time to cool off before making the call. Better yet, wait to speak to them in person.

311 When writing an e-mail, type out the person or persons names that are in the To: box in the head of the letter. Do not just start your e-mail with a sentence, and always sign your e-mails. If you have someone in the CC: box, do not address them in the e-mail. CC: means that you do not expect them to reply to the e-mail.

312 Stop expecting others to do things as well as you do. Face it, your standards are pretty high and you are good. Why would any employee do it better? This does not mean you lower your standards, this simply means that you accept a job that is well done.

313 Learn to manage your boss. This practice will make it easier for you to do your job. Ask your boss when it is best to communicate and how. Teach your staff to do the same thing with you.

314 Show that you care. Check in with employees when they are on the road. Be sure that they arrived safe and sound and that all is going well.

315 Be dangerous, and learn all the jobs in your team. Granted, you do not have to be able to do them well, but at least have a clue as to what is involved. This will help you replace the person if needed, and maybe even step in if necessary.

316 Build a B-team. Having a second string is critical to your success. Always have cross-training in place for all jobs. This may not require more staff, but it is vital when someone is sick for long periods of time.

317 Empower people to make decisions. Set boundaries and expect people to perform.

318 Contractors rock! Many people love the freedom of being a contractor. Make it an option for existing people if it fits the bill. Contractors can save you a ton of money.

319 Be sure all employees know your travel schedule. Make sure you are very clear about who is in charge while you are away. Set your auto e-mail reply and your office voice mail to direct calls and questions to the appropriate person while you are away.

320 Always be training your replacement. Sound dangerous? Not if you want to grow and move up "the ladder." Your boss cannot promote you if someone cannot step into your role.

321 Have you trained your replacement today? Job security is an old-school way of not allowing your team to grow. Your office should function like a well-oiled machine when you are away. If not, start training your team. When the day comes that they can live without you, you have stopped growing yourself. Always be improving the system, the process, and the people.

322 Christmas cards are easy, fast, and sweet. Write a nice note to each person and tell them how much you appreciate them and their contribution to the team.

323 Working from home can be a good option for some employees once a month. Give this some serious thought before making it an office-wide offer.

324 Know the rules from your HR department. Be aware of number of vacation days, how vacation time works, number of holidays, etc. Make time to know the rules. How can you enforce what you do not know?

325 401ks are very important. Why is it that less than 45% of the workforce contributes to 401k? Experts say it is because employees just do not know enough about the system. Take time to have the experts meet with your staff. Encourage them to contribute.

326 Take out a thank you ad in the paper. Near the holidays, I like to take out a thank you ad and thank each of my team by name. This means a ton to the people under you, and the world knows you care.

327 Angel trees and other charity funds are great around the holidays. Make it fun for your staff to get involved, but do not make it mandatory.

328 Do not call employees after hours with an issue, or you may risk ruining their night as they sweat about it. It is far better to bring it up the next day.

329 Work out or get more active. People respect those who respect themselves.

330 Working from home yields great results. This is a touchy topic, but one you cannot ignore. If the job can be done from home, encourage it one day per month.

331 Kids at home sick? So what! A well-equipped staff will not stop if a kid is home sick. Rather than miss a day at work, employees with the right equipment can just plug in and keep working.

332 Be wary of "wants" vs. "needs". Does the job require a computer with 4GB of RAM or is that a costly luxury? Will it truly increase productivity or will it make playing games at 4pm better? Get up to speed on what is required of the machines needed to get the job done.

333 Do not develop a "do as I say and not as I do" workplace. Work hard to fight this at all costs.

334 Take a smoke break. Every now and again, walk outside to the smoking area and chat with key people. Make it frequent so you do not seem out of place in the crowd.

335 Chat often with your employees. If the only time you speak to employees is during a business conversation, how do expect to get to know them at all? You cannot effectively manage an employee unless you know how they tick.

336 Visit employee cubicles after hours. Walk into an employee's cube and stand in the middle. Do not touch anything. Just stand there and look around. Look at everything, but touch nothing. You can learn a lot from just looking.

337 Set a clear deadline when you need something completed. If you set no deadline, do not expect the task to be done right away.

338 If you asked for something to be done for an upcoming meeting, tell the employees how much it meant that they did a nice job. If what they created does not get used, simply tell them that their contribution to the meeting was substantial.

339 Be careful how many times you ask for things at the last minute. While some people operate well under pressure, most do not. If you want the best work out of your team, give them the time to do great work.

340 Take the time to hire the right person. However, do not get behind waiting for Mr. Right. Many an old maid has gone to their grave lonely because Mr. Perfect did not appear. Having the right person on the team is critical, but not hiring anyone can be costly as well.

341 Make attending weddings a priority. These are very special times for your team, and your support is much appreciated. Give a very nice gift if you can afford it, and write them a special note to wish them luck.

342 Create an innovation awards program where employees are rewarded when recognized by other employees for great ideas.

343 Never leave long voicemails for your team. Face-to-face conversations are better because they allow employees to ask questions.

344 Put security measures in place to keep your work place safe. Get the team involved in the planning and decision-making.

345 Get the right people on the bus from the beginning of a project. Take your time in hiring, and be diligent to fire a person who is not meeting the needs that the job requires.

346 Periods of probation rarely work. Write up people when needed and fire when needed. If you get to a point where you need to put a person on probation, you should just move forward and fire the person.

347 Keep politics and religion out of the office. Be very clear regarding your policy about these issues.

348 Take employees on special business outings like a golf meeting with a vendor. Then, be sure to rotate the invites to others.

349 Showing favoritism is very apparent around the office. So, be very careful.

350 Do not manipulate a group to get them to agree with an unpopular decision.

351 Help your employees manage you by being very clear about your daily schedule.

352 Do not harass employees about issues as they walk in the door. Give them a chance to get to work and settle in before you unload.

353 Ask employees to tell you when they are leaving. A simple "see ya tomorrow" is fine. This encourages employees to check out, and you can keep better tabs on the time clock. However, this is far different than asking permission to leave for the day.

354 E-mail cannot convey the tone required to deliver a reprimand or punishment. Always address these issues in person or over the phone if you are separated from your employees by more than 100 miles.

355 Create a birthday exchange so that employees' birthdays are not missed. Here is how it works. Create a list of birthdays. The first birthday in January is responsible for the cake, etc. for the next birthday on the list. Have people on your team group the

birthdays. Birthdays are a simple, yet proactive way to encourage team morale.

356 Encourage flu shots. If your company does not offer a discount on flu shots demand it. This is one single step toward increased productivity. If your staff is ill, tell them to stay home. Set a good example by following your own advice here as well. You are not a super hero for coming to work sick; you are just super stupid.

357 When you make a request, be specific about the deadline. If it is not a rush, be sure to tell your employee that simple fact.

358 If you ask an employee to "hang out" and wait for your call, have the courtesy to call back if you are late, or if you are not going to need them after all.

359 Prepare a state-of-the-staff survey and ask some key questions. Have a senior level staff member conduct the survey and assure the staff of anonymity. Look at the results carefully and use them to grow personally. I call this taking the pulse of the staff.

360 Never be afraid to fire a "bad apple" even if they are in a revenue-generating role. On a yearly basis, take time to evaluate each employee's contribution to not only revenue, but overall morale as well. Doing an internal, confidential audit of employee morale is a great way to gauge this issue. I have often sent surveys to the production team and made the sales personnel bonuses based on what the surveys report.

361 Create a monthly lunch program wherein you take one employee per month out to lunch and chat about work and life. Be sure to tell them how important they are to the company. Schedule enough lunches to work in all employees. Do not keep this a secret, or you risk people feeling left out.

362 Take the time to say good-bye and thank you to each person who works under you.

363 Action plans for employees without follow-up and accountability are meaningless. Once-a-year reviews are about growth as much as they are about pointing out problem areas.

364 Create a yearly growth plan for all of the members of your team, and have it accompany their yearly reviews. Remember, good managers always want to be "growing" their replacement.

365 Build team-building sessions into your yearly budget. It is not expensive to have two team-building functions each year if you plan ahead. Any upper level manager who cuts out team-building money is not worth working for. Team-building is mission critical to your success and the success of your team.

Final Exam

QUESTION #1: Do you plan to change how you treat your team? If your answer is yes, give yourself 10 points. If your answer is no, give yourself 5 points.

Score: _____

QUESTION #2: Do you plan to get to know your team in a more personal way without getting "personal"? If your answer is no, give yourself 5 points. If your answer is yes, give yourself 10 points.

Score: _____

QUESTION #3: Do you plan to make your meetings more efficient and a place where you will talk less? If your answer is yes, give yourself 10 points. If your answer is no, give yourself 5 points.

Score: _____

QUESTION #4: Do you plan to leave your office door open more than it is closed? If your answer is yes, give yourself 10 points. If your answer is no, give yourself 5 points.

Score: _____

Now, add up your points....   Final Score: _____

SCORE:

20 or less: Get out of management.

25-30: You can do this, but it will require dedication.

35-40: Keep up the good work. Well done.

NOTE:
If you are using this book as a group training guide,
answer these questions on your own and
then discuss them as a group.
Be open, honest and SHARE.

About Ryan Dohrn

How To Be A Manager Without Being a Jerk offers 365 tips for becoming a better manager every day of the year. Written by nationally recognized speaker and teacher Ryan Dohrn, this book offers easy-to-understand management tips in a "quick read" format.

Dohrn was the youngest member of the management team at ABC TV in Chicago at only 26 years of age. He has compiled tips from good and bad managers in his career path to success. As an Internet guru who survived the dot-bomb crash of the late 1990's, Dohrn's ventures of success have been featured in USA Today, on Forbes.com and on numerous FOX, ABC and CBS affiliates across the nation. Dohrn is an Emmy award winning TV producer and now operates Brain Swell Media. He was born in Clinton, Iowa, is married and enjoys his two boys with his wife Andre' at their home in South Carolina.

Ryan's complete bio can be found online at
http://www.RyanDohrn.com

Other books from Ryan Dohrn:
How To Be A Christian Without Being A Jerk ©2007
How To Be A Parent Without Being A Jerk ©2007
How To Be A Coach Without Being A Jerk ©2007